WINDTHROW

WINDTHROW

K. A. Hays

Carnegie Mellon University Press
Pittsburgh 2017

ACKNOWLEDGMENTS

I would like to thank the editors of the following journals, in which these poems, some in altered form or under different titles, have appeared:

32 Poems: "Prediction"
American Literary Review: "Of Outrageous Fortune"
Beloit Poetry Journal: "And the Lord Hath Taken Away"
Cincinnati Review: "Dune's Testament," "Lake's Testament"
The Colorado Review: "In Heat," "Petition"
The Cortland Review: "I Asked the Flood, Are You Happy?"
Greensboro Review: "Skunk Cabbage Testament"
Gulf Coast: "Bicycling Ice Cream Man," "Radishes and Any Small Thing"
The Journal: "Mother Goose Testament"
jubilat: "To the Moth in the Phlox"
Kenyon Review: "Another Prophecy Unfulfilled," "On the Day the World Is Forecast
        to End and Does Not"
The Paris-American: "Windflaw," "Windthrow" [Some shudder]
Pleiades: "Of Happiness"
A Poetry Congeries: "Crow"
Puerto del Sol: "Of Grief"
Southern Humanities Review: "Mind in Flock, Mind Apart," "Or Only Here,
        Brambling," "But What Seems Fixed Slides Away"
Southern Poetry Review: "Easter"
The Southern Review: "Letter from Down the Shore"
Tin House: "Broadfork," "Heat Goes out Walking in the Cold"
Zocalo Public Square: "Water Lily"
Zone 3: "First Lesson"

"Prediction" appears in *The Book of Scented Things: An Anthology of Contemporary American Poetry* (2014). "In Heat" and "Heat Goes out Walking in the Cold" were reprinted on *Poetry Daily*, and "Mother Goose Self-Help" was reprinted on *Verse Daily*. I am grateful to many journal editors and friends for close readings and sound advice, and to Gerald Costanzo and Cynthia Lamb for their years of support.

Book design by Jennifer Huang

Library of Congress Control Number 2016948990
ISBN 978-0-88748-619-7

10   9   8   7   6   5   4   3   2   I

for you

*. . . winds or . . . hurricanes can bring down canopy-sized trees . . .
churning up the soil and . . . creating gaps in the forest . . . that permit
light to enter . . .*

—John Kricher, *A Field Guide to Eastern Forests*

Contents

I. Throw

Windthrow [When an oak leans]   11
Crow   12
Of Grief   13
Skunk Cabbage Testament   15
Wrack   16
Of Outrageous Fortune   17
I Asked the Flood, Are You Happy?   18
Windthrow [Last night's kindling]   19
On the Day the World Is Forecast to End and Does Not   20

II. Sow and Reap

First Lesson   23
Or Only Here, Brambling   24
Mother Goose Testament   25
Love before Love   27
Another Prophecy Unfulfilled   28
Easter   29
Crocus   30
Broadfork   31
Radishes and Any Small Thing   32
Windflaw   33
In Heat   34
Heat Goes out Walking in the Cold   35

III. WAVE

Dune's Testament   39
Letter from Down the Shore   40
Down the Shore Love Song   42
    1. Billboard at Sea   42
    2. One Sees the Image of Oneself, a Winner   43
    3. No, Not Really a New Life   44
    4. On User-Friendly Screens   45
    5. But Real Compared to What?   46
    6. Sign, Sign, Sign   47
    7. I Do, I Do Approve   48
    8. Long Ago, the Many Gods Dealt with Us Daily   49
Bicycling Ice Cream Man   50

IV. THROWN

Petition   53
Mind in Flock, Mind Apart   54
To the Moth in the Phlox   55
Lake's Testament   56
But What Seems Fixed Slides Away   58
Of Happiness   59
Water Lily   60
Some Thought of Purpose   61
And the Lord Hath Taken Away   62
Windthrow [Some shudder]   63
Prediction   64

I. THROW

Light takes the tree, but who can tell us how?

—Theodore Roethke

. . . are you saying I can
flourish, having no hope
of enduring?

—Louise Glück

WINDTHROW

When an oak leans   limbs
stripped   leaves spun
trunk creaking   bent
then snapping   so the root ball hurls
to the air's blaze   and what housed owls
teeths centipedes

soon   the sun puts palm to ground
soon   the woods go cherry   cherry
as from the aching foreheads of old gods

leap new gods   a bend
of saplings   laughing up
so why can't I say

Windthrow   go and come?
you   go and come

CROW

In the dun stumps
of shorn corn, the soil
ice-tinged, almost smeary,
a crow bobs, feasting.
Or not crow—rather
crow's shape cut
from the rough corn field,
behind which hangs a blackness
supple and true:
a blackness that was
before crow, or field,
or I. When the shape stills,
I could climb into it—
but, not wanting now
to sleep, I let
the shape again
go crow. So the husks
keep on dropping
from the beak.
So the earth goes on urging,
in spite of it,
a slow, brown thaw.

OF GRIEF

A crab the tide's flipped in
 scoots back to sea.

Some gull beaks her up
then hurls her back

to break on rocks,
split to the meat—

to fight with half a shell.
She goes clawless. Soon

the gull feeds. No beauty
in suffering. I want no art

as evidence. No metaphor,
no word, no thing—.

The ocean licks the lines, and a woman
bends: the crab's shell.

She holds it. Tosses it back.
A wave slinks over,

smooths out the lines
the crab dug—

and those lines fold
in a fist, in folds of land,

or in a fissure, some hole
in the heckled mind,

mind
that scuttles and turns,

in chill and heat, ridiculous,
toward sun.

SKUNK CABBAGE TESTAMENT

Then give us a bog.
Let the flowers come early.
Let us burn whitely through ice,
though we open
to a clouded sky.
Widen the leaves, thicken us,
so starving moths
go madly on their way.
If we won't be granted peace,
if our souls will not be kept,
splay the flowers. Let them breathe
so tall and wide they rob the air
of its terrors.
Let tongues spit us back hot and sour.
If we must, let us roil in the belly
of the hunter
as we have roiled
by the still waters,
and been sore afraid.

WRACK

When wrack's no more
      limp-slung on the rocks
but in the tide-surge, a cloudbank
      for the fishes riffling in,
I mope on
      about the coming ebb,
but when it comes,
      the wrack, heaped up
at the low hour,
      dries out (no grief, no praise).
And the sea sneaks back and buffs it,
      fills its bladders.
It ushers in a fickle thing.
      Sets out
a temporary feast. I guess
      that's the only kind.

Of Outrageous Fortune

Look to the rope, coiled and stacked
by lobster traps.
And to the buoy tethered to each trap.
The lobsters, too.
But not
the wrack (unworried
in more wrack)—
if heaved up with the lobster,
trapped, make me
as wrack, thrown off;
if thrown,
to float. Or tumble under.
To take in food.
If light, then light.
If suffering
the slings and arrows, say,
then slings.
Then arrows.

I Asked the Flood, Are You Happy?

I asked the flood,
Are you happy?
And the flood ran on mutely
with a flush of brown cheek
and a turned-away eye—
happiness
laying down no speech.

But the green light, buzzing,
spoke to the rush of sticks.
Told the flood, *Go.*

I did not ask the light,
Are you happy?
I became it.
The flood sallied forth,
pressed beneath me,
and I spoke yellow, then red,
then green again,

and was not happy.
And so became the flood.
And turned away.

WINDTHROW

for John Haines, 1924-2011

Last night's kindling   char-strung
shrugs off ash   steeps in the rock-ring
By the blow-downs   roots splayed

leaves burn through snow-swath   hold open
able hands   I can smell the past
that heats those roots   hums in the leaves

You dead   do you see   the wind's snuck off?
sun smoking low?   a slagged coal
that goes gladly? gladly goes?   Is that the calm

you said you were headed for?   Still
I crouch by the rocks   planning a night-fire
the kind the dumb living make   kicking up

another tender quarrel   a tomorrow and
a tomorrow   and

On the Day the World Is Forecast to End and Does Not

So night's been poured and drunk.
The migrained clouds stumble and blanch.
An ornery sky. A boring sun-slant on dingy snow.
On my own stoop, a Christmas wreath loses its skin—what dread
in the soft sleet-sound of needles settling on a mat.
                    But sun touches the porch—
the street stretches itself.
A junco cleans its breast in such light.
And it dips, it swoops, not into ruin—moves
to a truck stacked with cut trees, itself moving on some fated
or unfated errand. The trees—what gilding will come
to the trees. Not into ruin. Not into ruin now.

II. SOW AND REAP

The smallest sprout shows there is really no death . . .
All goes onward and outward, nothing collapsing . . .

—Walt Whitman

First Lesson

Look closer. The buds
have flooded with the blue to come,
and the grass itches with promise—
each blade, shaken, slurs its note
beneath the thoughtless grinding
of the spheres
(or music, as it is said)—

yes, the weeds are sick-green with all that is to be.

Only listen to the wind-bent spruce,
its static and squeak,
the spruce cones falling.
That is how much time loves you.

But sit on stone steps. In sun.
Near lamps that do not yet need
to be lit. Is this a way
to love time?

The wind on a soy field
does not love the soy,
but changes it,
such that a viewer might say,
How fine.
You can be that viewer. You can try
to be the cloud that lets go its shadow
on a green hill.

Or Only Here, Brambling

Along the fence rabble the berry canes
planted last summer—a tangled mess of red
and brown wiring, cracked leaf and thorned veins

that ferry no blood, the engine still. The dead
don't mind it. Long sleep. No work. When they go
the living stop. Strip sheets, remake the bed—

so I'll strip off these brambles, clear ground, sow
some easy seed. Marigolds? Sure. I may
forget planting things, forever mow

the lawn in diamond pattern, weed-whack the day
from shrill growth back to a neat square room
where—what? What if, left alone, by May

new canes have pushed up? I assume
death and berrylessness, barren ground, bad air.
May as well assume a bud. A bloom

that startles with its freshness. Good tilth. Days fair
as fruit. As berries. Enough to share.

MOTHER GOOSE TESTAMENT

Climb a spout. Run a clock.
If the dogs laugh to see,
turn away. Remember: they're dogs.

Turn your face from the man
who brings down the fastest pigs

from the sky. If you should fall,

may it not be far. If it is far, rain washing you out,
clocks striking every which way,
pick up your sticks, and, walking,

look for a spoon, a beggar's jags,
and bells for your toes to ring as you go,

reminding you: you go.

If you worry about life under a haystack
or a hill: marry a fiddler.
Or become one.

Find a bowl stronger
than that of the wise men of Gotham.
Set sail.

A lovely time, this: play fiddle
in your bowl on the sea.
Play until the strings break

and the bow wears.
At some point, then, let go the fiddle.

You will forget the mother songs,

the diddle-Hubbard-dings,
as you break and wear,
wear and fall,

your bowl cracked but whole,
your bowl shining and sinking.

It gets a little sad here.

But even here make of your sinking
and shining
a song—a home-again song,

if you can help it, and,
if not that, then a song to cry

at the locks, and rap
at the windows.

A crooked song.

LOVE BEFORE LOVE

Each wind has a name—Busy. Then.
      Each long by weeks and changing in the eyes.
            The wind and the names change.

I sit by my fire, a wind comes in,
      I give a chair to the wind.
            What comes tomorrow?

      Anything.

Sometimes I'm a cloud who lives
      by the sun. A cloud at the roofs
            of the clouds. Some love

goes up and down, a week. An eye.
      The wind is long and crisp. You.
         Take a chair.

ANOTHER PROPHECY UNFULFILLED

In the beginning, the dirt was teaberried—
snapped leaf saying *We*, a drift of mint.
And the trees, the fox, and the vole leafed out for years.
The vole would birth, and the teaberry would sleep and fruit
without and through the people.

Here, when the street cleaner shirrs, as it must, gladly,
shining brushes taking up the earth,
the feet of dirt, the just legs and knees of dirt
turn and run beyond the people.
(But will be sown with people, the people fruiting out for years.)

Elsewhere, teaberry hoists itself up, chews the crust,
wants more *We*. But the people say *I. I* say I.
And the sun seems to urge the people onward,
with the vole, the tree, the fox. Seems to offer itself.
It will not tell the people, *Sleep*. It will not need to—.

EASTER

Again the bleeding heart flashes out, the grasses
lush and over-dark. Again, unseen
in the high brush, the mockingbird makes its trinities
of imitation—jay, jay, jay,
wren, wren, wren—
and in repeating, names itself,
as April, in its repetitions, names itself.
The wild tulips not yet mown are calling
come, and come.
The fat bees do. To step into this freshness
is to veer towards ruin.
You too have climbed far enough
into the wild tulips
to sniff their decay.
But again, naming themselves as they do,
into the yellow calling, the bees go.

CROCUS

Now leaf-rot tents
the bulbs so well, the shoots
slip upward, whitely grope,
feed, and glow
like tentacled creatures
in a sea's trench,
and like those,
are not unhappy.
When in weeks
they gasp through
the leaf layer,
wind baffling
the ghost-growth,
and the sky's kind,
the petals wag and shrug
as if the trek were easy.
And so it becomes easy.
Always now, there is no other,
they lisp, mouths lazing.
Sparrows hear it,
heads cocked
by the purple grins.
Of heat, of wilt,
of clenching back to bulb—
no scowl, and the sparrows say,
in hunger, *Always now.*
No other, the stem says in sun,
as it said snaking up darkly
toward an Other
sun-rich and equally fine.

BROADFORK

Raised—squat lily's fingers,
crabapple's flush, bewildering day,
and eggs in soil. To take

and be taken,
I might heave a broadfork, strain,
and drop the teeth.

The past. Tines chew.
The tines turn it over.
The packed-down

not wintered under,
the fruits an idea
uncome.

Time puffs its chest
and here is its vision.

Radishes and Any Small Thing

Red seeds, pinched in
to ashed-over land,
then patted down,
put out
no wisdom—
just an emotionless tick
I can hear, a kind of
I am I am,
the being of which
mine could be part
(some days),
along with water, worm,
wind, the dust of minds
like mine, fattening up
the radishes
and any small thing
unmeant to be, and meaning.

WINDFLAW

Only the mundane middle-of-things
stays green   flamed by the brilliances

      (bud roused red   or broke-gold leaf)
      Blinking into   and flashing out

the hues squall   as the city soon-to-be sounds
like the city soon gone   and the just-born

      squint like the dying   See
      how the first leaf   wrinkled

unstrong   finds windflaw
and clings   then clinging

      having unpinked   wet
      and glad   goes bronze

In Heat

Now the yellowy angel stills
the swifts from their jabber and swoop,

soothes the air from the pear tree's highest boughs
to the shocks of plaintain

in the sidewalk cracks, crouched
without a stir.

Good silence she wills in late afternoon.
Good silence swaddled soon in the robin's weird devotions—

Cheer and *O.*

Even the power lines must buzz in praise.
And the sage, who droops for lack of rain,

bows green in deference.
The slip of borage opens blue and spreads.

Yes, she lies down thick in yellow blooms
that will be long fruits.

She sleeps among squash.
The mind dozes midday in awe of her.

It fears no end. Fears no persistence.
And the people wait like buds in her name.

HEAT GOES OUT WALKING IN THE COLD

for Karen Mapes, 1955-2013

It seems possible, and I've been told,
that even the dying, who don't mean to,
stow mint at the ribs,
at the liver the waft
of split tomatoes, and April's peas
wire and tendril up, unruly,
at the backs of the eyes.

The old story: Decembers,
fiddleheads unwind
in a cat's worn foot pads—
and far in a man's deaf ear
tug the brown wade
and gold peeping
of May ponds.

Hard to believe, most days,
that under the ice-tilted walks,
plantain aches yellowly, hums
in August air. Or that even
in the spine of a child
who grieves for her mother
wakes dame's rocket, unwilled,
gangly, soon
a sapling with the tough ears
of elephants.
That's the sapling the dead
blaze into, summer walking in winter.
Yes. In wind-wracked limbs,
the green wick thaws the core.

III. WAVE

Behind us,
the beach,
    yes, its

scrim,
  yes, of
   grass, dune, sky—Desire

goes by . . .

—Carl Phillips

DUNE'S TESTAMENT

And the beachgrass, blown
with dusty miller sprout,
the seaside goldenrod.
The beach pea. Each, in swaying,

speaks a prophecy. As wind scraped
the foredune, sowed
their seed, so wind too
will rake, wipe clean
in a blowout, scatter,
build a broad way.

An opening—
here, a bayberry pokes up,
a sumac, and an ivy—
all cling and curl.
All curl and cling to stay.
As if a thing could stay.

LETTER FROM DOWN THE SHORE

They've collapsed the bungalows that lined
the coast and put up condos. Now three families walk
and sleep and feast where there was one,
thank God (there's war, growth's good). In tall shelves
stacked with citizens, what strength against the cold
Iscariot sea, a block away—the sea that rocks

and rails against the boardwalk
where, for a hundred years, these shops have sold rock
candy, postcards, saltwater taffy, cold
carbonated drinks. Fudge. The shells
of moon snails. Alone by the sea, one
fisherman stands, his back to the lines

of us, the boardwalk crowd. He's perched on rock
half-steeped in mist. I watch him cast his line
and reel it in, then cast again. A storm, just one
of the endless squalls the sandy shelf
has seen, hurls in to hound his walk
back to the wooden steps. He's chosen this—the colder

view, the churning froth's uneasy lines
of curdling foam. A ravaged jetty rock
from which to fish. I want to know what causes one
to leave the happy yawn of bathers on the shallow shelf
and swim out past the breakers with the sea's confederate cold
for company. I've known fools who want to walk

to where the water rabbles structure, gives cold
end to disparate things. These drifters listen as they walk
to waves that do not count themselves and won't accumulate, but line
the afternoon with sounds repeated, so the splash and surge speak—*One, On*

and *One* again—and move one in and out, until one shelves
her needs, then loses sense of self, that rock

imperative to keep. And so these fools forget the hefty rocks
of progress, and accrual. They place them on a shelf
too high to reach. They pray for a hearer of prayers and mutter let us walk
without our feet and make homes between the lines
of fish and let us feel no fire and no wind—
just water. There are fools who want this sometimes. I am one.

Down the Shore Love Song

I. Billboard at Sea

The boat that holds the flashing screen
was built to be a fishing boat—
a boat of ever-open eyes
hauled up from salt and heave,
a boat of boot and hook and knotted line.
It beams from there
to our towels and chairs
some thoughts:
A muscled man. Bikinied girl. A shrimp.
Tonight at Harrod's: Zappa playing Zappa.

Past the Atlantic's swagger of fish,
chaos flung out, scraped back,
the screen boat soothes, lays its cool hand
on the forehead: the image of another boat,
a touring pleasure craft
for me, on shore, to ride.
On tour, I might glide by
the back of this same screen—
or glimpse the self, seated, among friends.
A towel across the lap, the head reclined,
a picture of the ease I'm here to find.

2. ONE SEES THE IMAGE OF ONESELF, A WINNER

No depth of current,
fish-glide and swallow,
cloud of driven sand,
whale-rumble and torn reef—
think of Atlantic City:
the pleasure
of a machine
into which one drops a quarter
and out spills a new life.

3. No, Not Really a New Life

Tomorrow, yesterday—
a gull, some kids at play:
a game of catch in which the ball
is lost. Then found!
Then lost again. The eye
predicts next week
and year: a wave
of astounding height!
Now I spy the fin of a dolphin—tomorrow!
Tomorrow: the spout of an unspottable whale.

4. On User-Friendly Screens

Our closest friends may read that we are here,
and show approval
with the movement
of a thumb.
Their liking crisps the jetty,
makes cloud-shapes more discernible,
the bile-taste of sea
more real.

5. But Real Compared to What?

It's possible the screen boat never was
a fishing boat.
It may be made to seem
to have been.
Sure, I give a nod to the screen boat.
Don't I too suggest I am
a thing from some one place and time?
To this the screen boat nods
to me a Somer's Point buffet.

6. SIGN, SIGN, SIGN

Two green flags show where to swim.
The sign says after 8 p.m.
the ocean's closed.
We gossip and lounge, push and pull the feet,
mimic tides, machines that rip the land.
The smallest alteration to the sand,
when I make it, satisfies a need—
and seeing other pairs of feet that pat
and drag the form of things, I do approve.

7. I Do, I Do Approve

Meanwhile some military jet, droning over,
rattles my chair and snores off past the tilt
of my umbrella.
Meanwhile a mockingbird, gray in the dune grass,
keeps lifting her wings, flashing white bars,
then folding them back, as if imagining
some noble flight not to be made.

8. Long Ago, the Many Gods Dealt with Us Daily

But what good came of that?
Terrors kill us off, storms bully through,
some virus, some war—some wind, or just a breeze
jerks to a gust,
clouds chuff in, thunder behind,
and the terns streak off
to whatever terny place they go.
We beachgoers stand,
dust off the thighs,
hair whipped with beachgrass, bent
cottonwoods, flags
and fencing at the dunes.
Some hold the hands
of sandy children.
Some hoist up totes.
I turn my back to the shore,
but still turn back once more and look again,
and raise an arm, a screen,
as if I could hold the sea.
That old wine-dark sea.

Bicycling Ice Cream Man

When the dunes spool down
to shoreline his shaken bell's call,
and kids run toward him, fisting
damp bills, feet seared
by the hot-sand dash,

a gull picks up
from their path, hovers
and bobs, its gray shade-shape
gone smaller and going
like an unnamed dread—

just so, grief can be startled away
by a stranger's raised arm, or the idea
of a cooler stocked with ice.
Some stranger is always holding a bell.
Some ideas keep ringing.

IV. THROWN

Not as oneself did one find rest . . .

—Virginia Woolf

I know no speck so troublesome as self.

—George Eliot

PETITION

Here floats the mind on summer's dock.
The knees loose up, hands dither off,
the eyes have never heard of clocks.
The mind won't feel the hours, the mind spreads wide
among the hours, wide in sun. Dear sun,
who gives the vision but is not the vision.
Who is the body and the bodies
that speak into the dark below the dock.
Who to the minnows in the sand-sunk tire
seems like love.
Make us the brightness bent through shade.
The thing, or rush of things, that makes
an opening, a way.

MIND IN FLOCK, MIND APART

They scatter high, the grackles. What's to know
of mind in flock? Some baffling drive to share?
I keep apart my thought. They swoop and go

as if some harried god inhaled. A show
of beauty, then—the great lung thrills with air
that scatters high the grackles. This I know:

they perch like thorns, that blackened croaking row
along a bough. We too sing what we bear,
but keep apart most thoughts—they swoop and go

like hawks, drab hunters circling, circling slow
over small things: to dive, to feed. To tear
and scatter high. The grackles (those I know)

stay close in hunger: flit down, grub low,
blue clucks, green squeals—and each self gone where?
Not kept apart. Less thought, more swoop and go—

a particle, a wave. The peppered dusk. But no,
what weird squalling—is what's here in me out there?
They scatter high, the grackles, what I know.
They keep a part of thought. I swoop—they go.

TO THE MOTH IN THE PHLOX

To the moth in the phlox   the monarch's feet fall hard.
The swallow's a white archer   curling sharp.

No cloud's a cloud—   just light or stronger light.
The sun's unstill in the moth,   who, skipping, knows
the blur of root with rock   and dust with day.

To the moth the day is pollen,   violet lips
held open for the take.   And time's the bank
of monarchs and quick birds   through which to jink:

a sidelong motion, cracked,   over the phlox.
Pink petalled and fast winged,   the bank's at play.

LAKE'S TESTAMENT

When the boats sail, I let them.
I will not trouble their passing—
passage of boats more quiet than boats at rest
(clap-slapping on the face of me).
I make their going quiet. I let it be.

The Loud Ones don't hear—not mosses furring the bank,
green pucker, brown crawl. Not minnows' sneak,
or the blue liftings wind makes on the skin.
The Loud Ones say, *Hurt*. No hurt.
I hear the damselfly
lowering the nail of herself
to the shore.
Taking in my sun.

Nights the Loud Ones say *Scare*.
They can't see the rich un-light
beneath the docks, circling out.
Or the fine dark seam
that binds me to the rest of things.
And nights are mine too as much as sun.

A fish eats a fish. No *scare* in it,
Blue, red—a part of me that swells,
then falls.
When the aspens drop yellow wings,
the umbrellas, closed on the docks, tell
how the heat felt when the Loud sat beneath,
dipping and flexing their toes—

I do not love the Loud Ones, do not miss them
when they go, winters, no, not the lures or midges

or the unfeelable hurts they shriek over—
splinter, push, dunk. Their laughings.
I take them when they are given.
I take the boats at rest in cold, given,
and hold them, the boat and I one
to make the cold passing quiet. To let it be.

But What Seems Fixed Slides Away

No current—none to see but the flat doze
of brackish muck where bugs eddy and feed.
The only motion my gray wade. Then come
the deerflies in giddy chaotic loops and dives.
I thought the water had no flow, but now
the grasses, lisping north, say, *No,*
we tongues flap yellow in the mouth as one.
There's pull in the fuzzed gut of what is not
becoming but has been and is a flow.
Algae strung on the rush-root breathes a fast
insistence, quickening down there until
around a bend the water's white on rocks
and sounds the strength that bows the roots of lilies,
that yanks them out. Pale crowns. I too am thrown.

OF HAPPINESS

In rain the child says the lake has a sad face.
The child shows the mother. Look.
But though the mother walks the dock,

and paddles a boat,
the lake turns its face broad to the child,
so only the child sees the shown

face of it. When the lake's in sun
the mother says the lake is happy, but
the child is cheerful. The child says no—

the lake is happy and the lake is sad.
And the mother doesn't see
until the child, tossing water

from a bucket into the lake, says,
Oh. Now the face is happy and the face is gone.

WATER LILY

One isn't one only.
That much is sure—

beneath the lance-leaves
and the scum,

the wiring tangles into one engine,
same humming ages back,

fat with the flower to come,
fat with the flowers before,

so petals split,
redden at the clench.

Red that says *Here*, and *Be*.
That says *Come*.

This too danders,
spills dust, films over.

The fish know. The eggs
of flies. In widening,

a lily mouths its dirge
in praise of now.

SOME THOUGHT OF PURPOSE

When the creek greened over
        the creek saw its girth
                and things such girth could hold,
such as crayfish
        and the glad rocks
                and the rocks who
despair of themselves,
        tumbling like fishes
                after some thought
of purpose beyond
        taking part in time.
                And these despairing rocks
the creek felt for,
        having despaired of itself long ago
                before taking a view
of itself as carried along
        and carrying,
                with tenderness,
the confused despair
        and joy of a couple
                of creekly things.

AND THE LORD HATH TAKEN AWAY

The bee claws into touch-me-nots,
the mouth a flame against the orange of it.
And the mind stops its minding.
The legs hold up the butt end
to the flower. *Why not stay?*
the bee asks as the dusk comes.
Why not stay inside the orange mouth
above the fleabane, balling up
inside a horn of plenty. Mornings I find
such bees. Half in, half out.
The body in the mouth from which it drank.
Morning night-damp still. I shake the bush
of touch-me-nots, I make a blaze of them
against the cold. The bee holds fast, is drunk.

WINDTHROW

Some shudder   some go without fear
Soon dirt skips up   laurel frilling
the downed one   Yes   time too

bunches and waves   pressed
as from the thrown   seeds shed casings
slip out   hello

heat whipping to cold   the clouds bloated
to rumble and clot   to tarry
panting   speaking in tongues

yes   happy as I
or as you   small one
Now the sapling   born of the giant

who is the giant   climbs on
drinking   digging in
Come then   here

PREDICTION

Hyacinthoides non-scripta

Now the brook's a swell
of melt in purpled shade.
A prophecy
greens up along the bank,
puts out fists,
then nods and broods.
I'd be the bee come from beneath.
And from above, rain's slung to a bud,
and the sun's puddled, the towhee,
spring-thin, calling Drink.
Under a sweep of creek,
all valleys, mouths, and hands to be
ball up and do. They drink.
One body bulbed under
and another to come.
A still bell. Soon rung.